The Ugly Du

A Play

A. A. Milne

Samuel French - London
New York - Toronto - Hollywood

CHARACTERS

The King.
The Queen.
The Princess Camilla
The Chancellor.
Dulcibella.
Prince Simon.
Carlo.

THE UGLY DUCKLING

The Scene is the Throne Room of the Palace ; a room of many doors, or, if preferred, curtain-openings : simply furnished with three thrones for Their Majesties and Her Royal Highness the PRINCESS CAMILLA— in other words, with three handsome chairs. At each side is a long seat : reserved, as it might be, for His Majesty's Council (if any), but useful, as to-day, for other purposes. The KING is asleep in his throne with a handkerchief over his face. He is a king of any country from any story-book, in whatever costume you please. But he should be wearing his crown.

A VOICE (*announcing*). His Excellency the Chancellor !

(*The* CHANCELLOR, *an elderly man in horn-rimmed spectacles, enters, bowing. The* KING *wakes up with a start and removes the handkerchief from his face.*)

KING (*with simple dignity*). I was thinking.

CHANCELLOR (*bowing*). Never, Your Majesty, was greater need for thought than now.

KING. That's what I was thinking. (*He struggles into a more dignified position.*) Well, what is it ? More trouble ?

CHANCELLOR. What we might call the old trouble, Your Majesty.

KING. It's what I was saying last night to the Queen. " Uneasy lies the head that wears a crown," was how I put it.

CHANCELLOR. A profound and original thought, which may well go down to posterity.

7

KING. You mean it may go down well with posterity. I hope so. Remind me to tell you some time of another little thing I said to Her Majesty : something about a fierce light beating on a throne. Posterity would like that, too. Well, what is it ?

CHANCELLOR. It is in the matter of Her Royal Highness' wedding.

KING. Oh . . . yes.

CHANCELLOR. As Your Majesty is aware, the young Prince Simon arrives to-day to seek Her Royal Highness' hand in marriage. He has been travelling in distant lands and, as I understand, has not—er—has not——

KING. You mean he hasn't heard anything.

CHANCELLOR. It is a little difficult to put this tactfully, Your Majesty.

KING. Do your best, and I will tell you afterwards how you got on.

CHANCELLOR. Let me put it this way. The Prince Simon will naturally assume that Her Royal Highness has the customary—so customary as to be, in my own poor opinion, slightly monotonous—has what one might call the inevitable—so inevitable as to be, in my opinion again, almost mechanical—will assume that she has the, as *I* think of it, faultily faultless, icily regular, splendidly——

KING. What you are trying to say in the fewest words possible is that my daughter is not beautiful.

CHANCELLOR. Her beauty is certainly elusive, Your Majesty.

KING. It is. It has eluded you, it has eluded me, it has eluded everybody who has seen her. It even eluded the Court Painter. His last words were, " Well, I did my best." His successor is now painting the view across the water-meadows from the West Turret. He says that his doctor has advised him to keep to landscape.

CHANCELLOR. It is unfortunate, Your Majesty, but there it is. One just cannot understand how it can have occurred.

KING. You don't think she takes after *me*, at all ? You don't detect a likeness ?

CHANCELLOR. Most certainly not, Your Majesty.

KING. Good. . . . Your predecessor did.

CHANCELLOR. I have often wondered what happened to my predecessor.

KING. Well, now you know. (*There is a short silence.*)

CHANCELLOR. Looking at the bright side, although Her Royal Highness is not, strictly speaking, beautiful——

KING. Not, truthfully speaking, beautiful——

CHANCELLOR. Yet she has great beauty of character.

KING. My dear Chancellor, we are not considering Her Royal Highness' character, but her chances of getting married. You observe that there is a distinction.

CHANCELLOR. Yes, Your Majesty.

KING. Look at it from the suitor's point of view. If a girl is beautiful, it is easy to assume that she has, tucked away inside her, an equally beautiful character. But it is impossible to assume that an unattractive girl, however elevated in character, has, tucked away inside her, an equally beautiful face. That is, so to speak, not where you want it—tucked away.

CHANCELLOR. Quite so, Your Majesty.

KING. This doesn't, of course, alter the fact that the Princess Camilla is quite the nicest person in the Kingdom.

CHANCELLOR (*enthusiastically*). She is indeed, Your Majesty. (*Hurriedly.*) With the exception, I need hardly say, of Your Majesty—and Her Majesty.

KING. Your exceptions are tolerated for their loyalty and condemned for their extreme fatuity.

CHANCELLOR. Thank you, Your Majesty.

KING. As an adjective for your King, the word

" nice " is ill-chosen. As an adjective for Her Majesty, it is—ill-chosen.

(*At which moment* HER MAJESTY *comes in. The* KING *rises. The* CHANCELLOR *puts himself at right angles.*)

QUEEN (*briskly*). Ah. Talking about Camilla ? (*She sits down.*)

KING (*returning to his throne*). As always, my dear, you are right.

QUEEN (*to* CHANCELLOR). This fellow, Simon—— What's he like ?

CHANCELLOR. Nobody has seen him, Your Majesty.

QUEEN. How old is he ?

CHANCELLOR. Five-and-twenty, I understand.

QUEEN. In twenty-five years he must have been seen by somebody.

KING (*to the* CHANCELLOR). Just a fleeting glimpse.

CHANCELLOR. I meant, Your Majesty, that no detailed report of him has reached this country, save that he has the usual personal advantages and qualities expected of a Prince, and has been travelling in distant and dangerous lands.

QUEEN. Ah ! Nothing gone wrong with his eyes ? Sunstroke or anything ?

CHANCELLOR. Not that I am aware of, Your Majesty. At the same time, as I was venturing to say to His Majesty, Her Royal Highness' character and disposition are so outstandingly——

QUEEN. Stuff and nonsense. You remember what happened when we had the Tournament of Love last year.

CHANCELLOR. I was not myself present, Your Majesty. I had not then the honour of—I was abroad, and never heard the full story.

QUEEN. No ; it was the other fool. They all rode up to Camilla to pay their homage—it was the first time they had seen her. The heralds blew their trumpets, and announced that she would marry whichever Prince was left master of the field when all but one had been unhorsed. The trumpets were blown again, they charged enthusiastically into the fight, and——

(*The* KING *looks nonchalantly at the ceiling and whistles a few bars.*)

—don't do that.

KING. I'm sorry, my dear.

QUEEN (*to* CHANCELLOR). And what happened? They all simultaneously fell off their horses and assumed a posture of defeat.

KING. One of them was not quite so quick as the others. I was very quick. I proclaimed him the victor.

QUEEN. At the Feast of Betrothal held that night——

KING. We were all very quick.

QUEEN. The Chancellor announced that by the laws of the country the successful suitor had to pass a further test. He had to give the correct answer to a riddle.

CHANCELLOR. Such undoubtedly is the fact, Your Majesty.

KING. There are times for announcing facts, and times for looking at things in a broadminded way. Please remember that, Chancellor.

CHANCELLOR. Yes, Your Majesty.

QUEEN. I invented the riddle myself. Quite an easy one. What is it which has four legs and barks like a dog? The answer is, "A dog."

KING (*to* CHANCELLOR). You see that?

CHANCELLOR. Yes, Your Majesty.

KING. It isn't difficult.

QUEEN. He, however, seemed to find it so. He said an eagle. Then he said a serpent; a very high mountain with slippery sides; two peacocks; a moonlight night; the day after to-morrow——

KING. Nobody could accuse him of not trying.

QUEEN. *I* did.

KING. I *should* have said that nobody could fail

to recognize in his attitude an appearance of doggedness.

QUEEN. Finally he said " Death." I nudged the King——

KING. Accepting the word " nudge " for the moment, I rubbed my ankle with one hand, clapped him on the shoulder with the other, and congratulated him on the correct answer. He disappeared under the table, and, personally, I never saw him again.

QUEEN. His body was found in the moat next morning.

CHANCELLOR. But what was he doing in the moat, Your Majesty ?

KING. Bobbing about. Try not to ask needless questions.

CHANCELLOR. It all seems so strange.

QUEEN. What does ?

CHANCELLOR. That Her Royal Highness, alone of all the Princesses one has ever heard of, should lack that invariable attribute of Royalty, supreme beauty.

QUEEN (to the KING). That was your Great-Aunt Malkin. She came to the christening. You know what she said.

KING. It was cryptic. Great-Aunt Malkin's besetting weakness. She came to *my* christening—she was one hundred and one then, and that was fifty-one years ago. (To the CHANCELLOR.) How old would that make her ?

CHANCELLOR. One hundred and fifty-two, Your Majesty.

KING (after thought). About that, yes. She promised me that when I grew up I should have all the happiness which my wife deserved. It struck me at the time—well, when I say " at the time," I was only a week old—but it did strike me as soon as anything could strike me—I mean of that nature —well, work it out for yourself, Chancellor. It opens up a most interesting field of speculation. Though naturally I have not liked to go into it at all deeply with Her Majesty.

QUEEN. I never heard anything less cryptic. She was wishing you extreme happiness.

KING. I don't think she was *wishing* me anything. However.

CHANCELLOR (*to the* QUEEN). But what, Your Majesty, did she wish Her Royal Highness ?

QUEEN. Her other godmother—on my side—had promised her the dazzling beauty for which all the women in my family are famous——

(*She pauses, and the* KING *snaps his fingers surreptitiously in the direction of the* CHANCELLOR.)

CHANCELLOR (*hurriedly*). Indeed, yes, Your Majesty. (*The* KING *relaxes.*)

QUEEN. And Great-Aunt Malkin said—(*to the* KING)—what were the words ?

KING.   I give you with this kiss
            A wedding-day surprise.
         Where ignorance is bliss
            'Tis folly to be wise.

I thought the last two lines rather neat. But what it *meant*——

QUEEN. We can all see what it meant. She was given beauty—and where is it ? Great-Aunt Malkin took it away from her. The wedding-day surprise is that there will never be a wedding day.

KING. Young men being what they are, my dear, it would be much more surprising if there *were* a wedding day. So how——

(*The* PRINCESS *comes in. She is young, happy, healthy, but not beautiful. Or let us say that by some trick of make-up or arrangement of hair she seems plain to us : unlike the* PRINCESS *of the story-books.*)

PRINCESS (*to the* KING). Hallo, darling ! (*Seeing the others.*) Oh, I say ! Affairs of state ? Sorry.

KING (*holding out his hand*). Don't go, Camilla. (*She takes his hand.*)

CHANCELLOR. Shall I withdraw, Your Majesty ?

QUEEN. You are aware, Camilla, that Prince Simon arrives to-day ?

PRINCESS. He has arrived. They're just letting down the drawbridge.

KING (*jumping up*). Arrived ! I must——

PRINCESS. Darling, you know what the drawbridge is like. It takes at *least* half an hour to let it down.

KING (*sitting down*). It wants oil. (*To the* CHANCELLOR.) Have *you* been grudging it oil ?

PRINCESS. It wants a new drawbridge, darling.

CHANCELLOR. Have I Your Majesty's permission——

KING. Yes, yes.

(*The* CHANCELLOR *bows and goes out.*)

QUEEN. You've told him, of course ? It's the only chance.

KING. Er—no. I was just going to, when——

QUEEN. Then I'd better. (*She goes to the door.*) You can explain to the girl ; I'll have her sent to you. You've told Camilla ?

KING. Er—no. I was just going to, when——

QUEEN. Then you'd better tell her now.

KING. My dear, are you sure——

QUEEN. It's the only chance left. (*Dramatically to heaven.*) My daughter ! (*She goes out.*)

(*There is a little silence when she is gone.*)

KING. Camilla, I want to talk seriously to you about marriage.

PRINCESS. Yes, father.

KING. It is time that you learnt some of the facts of life.

PRINCESS. Yes, father.

KING. Now the great fact about marriage is that once you're married you live happy ever after. All our history books affirm this.

PRINCESS. And your own experience too, darling.

KING (*with dignity*). Let us confine ourselves to history for the moment.

PRINCESS. Yes, father.

KING. Of course, there *may* be an exception here and there, which, as it were, proves the rule ; just as—oh, well, never mind.

PRINCESS (*smiling*). Go on, darling. You were going to say that an exception here and there proves the rule that all princesses are beautiful.

KING. Well—leave that for the moment. The point is that it doesn't matter *how* you marry, or *who* you marry, as long as you *get* married. Because you'll be happy ever after in any case. Do you follow me so far ?

PRINCESS. Yes, father.

KING. Well, your mother and I have a little plan——

PRINCESS. Was that it, going out of the door just now ?

KING. Er—yes. It concerns your waiting-maid.

PRINCESS. Darling, I have several.

KING. Only one that leaps to the eye, so to speak. The one with the—well, with everything.

PRINCESS. Dulcibella ?

KING. That's the one. It is our little plan that at the first meeting she should pass herself off as the Princess—a harmless ruse, of which you will find frequent record in the history books—and allure Prince Simon to his—that is to say, bring him up to the—— In other words, the wedding will take place immediately afterwards, and as quietly as possible—well, naturally in view of the fact that your Aunt Malkin is one hundred and fifty-two; and since you will be wearing the family bridal veil —which is no doubt how the custom arose—the surprise after the ceremony will be his. Are you following me at all ? Your attention seems to be wandering.

PRINCESS. I was wondering why you needed to tell me.

KING. Just a precautionary measure, in case you happened to meet the Prince or his attendant before

the ceremony ; in which case, of course, you would
pass yourself off as the maid——

PRINCESS. A harmless ruse, of which, also, you
will find frequent record in the history books.

KING. Exactly. But the occasion need not arise.

A VOICE (*announcing*). The woman Dulcibella !

KING. Ah ! (*To the* PRINCESS.) Now, Camilla,
if you will just retire to your own apartments, I will
come to you there when we are ready for the actual
ceremony.

(*He leads her out as he is talking ; and as he returns
calls out.*)

Come in, my dear !

(DULCIBELLA *comes in. She is beautiful, but dumb.*)

Now don't be frightened, there is nothing to be
frightened about. Has Her Majesty told you what
you have to do ?

DULCIBELLA. Y-yes, Your Majesty.

KING. Well now, let's see how well you can do
it. You are sitting here, we will say. (*He leads her
to a seat.*) Now imagine that I am Prince Simon.
(*He curls his moustache and puts his stomach in. She
giggles.*) You are the beautiful Princess Camilla
whom he has never seen. (*She giggles again.*) This
is a serious moment in your life, and you will find
that a giggle will not be helpful. (*He goes to the
door.*) I am announced : " His Royal Highness
Prince Simon ! " That's me being announced. Remember what I said about giggling. You should
have a far-away look upon the face. (*She does her
best.*) Farther away than that. (*She tries again.*)
No, that's too far. You are sitting there, thinking
beautiful thoughts—in maiden meditation, fancy-free,
as I remember saying to Her Majesty once . . .
speaking of somebody else . . . fancy-free, but with
the mouth definitely shut—that's better. I advance
and fall upon one knee. (*He does so.*) You extend
your hand graciously—*graciously ;* you're not trying

to push him in the face—that's better, and I raise
it to my lips—so—and I kiss it—(*he kisses it warmly*)
—no, perhaps not so ardently as that, more like this
(*he kisses it again*), and I say, " Your Royal Highness,
this is the most—er—— Your Royal Highness, I
shall ever be—no—— Your Royal Highness, it is
the proudest——" Well, the point is that *he* will say
it, and it will be something complimentary, and then
he will take your hand in both of his, and press it
to his heart. (*He does so.*) And then—what do *you*
say ?

DULCIBELLA. Coo !

KING. No, *not* Coo.

DULCIBELLA. Never had anyone do *that* to me
before.

KING. That also strikes the wrong note. What
you want to say is, " Oh, Prince Simon ! " . . .
Say it.

DULCIBELLA (*loudly*). Oh, Prince Simon !

KING. No, no. You don't need to shout until he
has said " What ? " two or three times. Always
consider the possibility that he *isn't* deaf. Softly,
and giving the words a dying fall, letting them play
around his head like a flight of doves.

DULCIBELLA (*still a little over-loud*). O-o-o-o-h,
Prinsimon !

KING. Keep the idea in your mind of a flight of
doves rather than a flight of panic-stricken elephants,
and you will be all right. Now I'm going to get up,
and you must, as it were, *waft* me into a seat by your
side. (*She starts wafting.*) *Not* rescuing a drowning
man, that's another idea altogether, useful at times,
but at the moment inappropriate. Wafting. Prince
Simon will put the necessary muscles into play—all
you require to do is to indicate by a gracious move-
ment of the hand the seat you require him to take.
Now ! (*He gets up, a little stiffly, and sits next to her.*)
That was better. Well, here we are. Now, I think
you give me a look : something, let us say, half-way
between the breathless adoration of a nun and the

voluptuous abandonment of a woman of the world; with an undertone of regal dignity, touched, as it were, with good comradeship. Now try that. (*She gives him a vacant look of bewilderment.*) Frankly, that didn't quite get it. There was just a little something missing. An absence, as it were, of all the qualities I asked for, and in their place an odd resemblance to an unsatisfied fish. Let us try to get at it another way. Dulcibella, have you a young man of your own?

DULCIBELLA (*eagerly, seizing his hand*). Oo, yes, he's ever so smart, he's an archer, well not as you might say a real archer, he works in the armoury, but old Bottlenose, *you* know who I mean, the Captain of the Guard, says the very next man they ever has to shoot, my Eg shall take his place, knowing Father and how it is with Eg and me, and me being maid to Her Royal Highness and can't marry me till he's a real soldier, but ever so loving, and funny like, the things he says, I said to him once, " Eg," I said——

KING (*getting up*). I rather fancy, Dulcibella, that if you think of Eg all the time, *say* as little as possible, and, when thinking of Eg, see that the mouth is not more than partially open, you will do very well. I will show you where you are to sit and wait for His Royal Highness. (*He leads her out. On the way he is saying*) Now remember—*waft—waft—* not *hoick*.

(PRINCE SIMON *wanders in from the back unannounced. He is a very ordinary-looking young man in rather dusty clothes. He gives a deep sigh of relief as he sinks into the* KING'S *throne*. . . .

CAMILLA, *a new and strangely beautiful* CAMILLA, *comes in*.)

PRINCESS (*surprised*). Well!
PRINCE. Oh, hallo!
PRINCESS. Ought you?
PRINCE (*getting up*). Do sit down, won't you?

PRINCESS. Who are you, and how did you get here ?

PRINCE. Well, that's rather a long story. Couldn't we sit down ? You could sit here if you liked, but it isn't very comfortable.

PRINCESS. That is the King's Throne.

PRINCE. Oh, is that what it is ?

PRINCESS. Thrones are not meant to be comfortable.

PRINCE. Well, I don't know if they're meant to be, but they certainly aren't.

PRINCESS. Why were you sitting on the King's Throne, and who are you ?

PRINCE. My name is Carlo.

PRINCESS. Mine is Dulcibella.

PRINCE. Good. And now couldn't we sit down ?

PRINCESS (*sitting down on the long seat to the left of the throne, and, as it were, wafting him to a place next to her*). You may sit here, if you like. Why are you so tired ? (*He sits down.*)

PRINCE. I've been taking very strenuous exercise.

PRINCESS. Is that part of the long story ?

PRINCE. It is.

PRINCESS (*settling herself*). I love stories.

PRINCE. This isn't a story really. You see, I'm attendant on Prince Simon, who is visiting here.

PRINCESS. Oh ? I'm attendant on Her Royal Highness.

PRINCE. Then you know what he's here for.

PRINCESS. Yes.

PRINCE. She's very beautiful, I hear.

PRINCESS. Did you hear that ? Where have you been lately ?

PRINCE. Travelling in distant lands—with Prince Simon.

PRINCESS. Ah ! All the same, I don't understand. Is Prince Simon in the Palace now ? The drawbridge *can't* be down yet !

PRINCE. I don't suppose it is. *And* what a noise it makes coming down !

PRINCESS. Isn't it terrible ?

PRINCE. I couldn't stand it any more. I just had to get away. That's why I'm here.

PRINCESS. But how ?

PRINCE. Well, there's only one way, isn't there ? That beech tree, and then a swing and a grab for the battlements, and don't ask me to remember it all—— (*He shudders.*)

PRINCESS. You mean you came across the moat by that beech tree ?

PRINCE. Yes. I got so tired of hanging about.

PRINCESS. But it's terribly dangerous !

PRINCE. That's why I'm so exhausted. Nervous shock. (*He lies back and breathes loudly.*)

PRINCESS. Of course, it's different for *me*.

PRINCE (*sitting up*). Say that again. I must have got it wrong.

PRINCESS. It's different for me, because I'm used to it. Besides, I'm so much lighter.

PRINCE. You don't mean that *you*——

PRINCESS. Oh yes, often.

PRINCE. And I thought I was a brave man ! At least, I didn't until five minutes ago, and now I don't again.

PRINCESS. Oh, but you are ! And I think it's wonderful to do it straight off the first time.

PRINCE. Well, *you* did.

PRINCESS. Oh no, not the first time. When I was a child.

PRINCE. You mean that you crashed ?

PRINCESS. Well, you only fall into the moat.

PRINCE. Only ! Can you *swim* ?

PRINCESS. Of course.

PRINCE. So you swam to the castle walls, and yelled for help, and they fished you out and walloped you. And next day you tried again. Well, if *that* isn't pluck——

PRINCESS. Of course I didn't. I swam back, and did it at once ; I mean I tried again at once. It wasn't until the third time that I actually did it. You see, I was afraid I might lose my nerve.

PRINCE. Afraid she might lose her nerve!

PRINCESS. There's a way of getting over from this side, too; a tree grows out from the wall and you jump into another tree—I don't think it's quite so easy.

PRINCE. Not quite so easy. Good. You must show me.

PRINCESS. Oh, I will.

PRINCE. Perhaps it might be as well if you taught me how to swim first. I've often heard about swimming, but never——

PRINCESS. You can't swim?

PRINCE. No. Don't look so surprised. There are a lot of other things which I can't do. I'll tell you about them as soon as you have a couple of years to spare.

PRINCESS. You can't swim and yet you crossed by the beech-tree! And you're *ever* so much heavier than I am! Now who's brave?

PRINCE (*getting up*). You keep talking about how light you are. I must see if there's anything in it. Stand up! (*She stands obediently and he picks her up.*) You're right, Dulcibella. I could hold you here for ever. (*Looking at her.*) You're very lovely. Do you know how lovely you are?

PRINCESS. Yes. (*She laughs suddenly and happily.*)

PRINCE. Why do you laugh?

PRINCESS. Aren't you tired of holding me?

PRINCE. Frankly, yes. I exaggerated when I said I could hold you for ever. When you've been hanging by the arms for ten minutes over a very deep moat, wondering if it's too late to learn how to swim—(*he puts her down*)—what I meant was that I should *like* to hold you for ever. Why did you laugh?

PRINCESS. Oh, well, it was a little private joke of mine.

PRINCE. If it comes to that, I've got a private joke too. Let's exchange them.

PRINCESS. Mine's very private. One other woman in the whole world knows, and that's all.

PRINCE. Mine's just as private. One other man knows, and that's all.

PRINCESS. What fun. I love secrets. . . . Well, here's mine. When I was born, one of my godmothers promised that I should be very beautiful.

PRINCE. How right she was.

PRINCESS. But the other one said this :

I give you with this kiss
A wedding-day surprise.
Where ignorance is bliss
'Tis folly to be wise.

And nobody knew what it meant. And I grew up very plain. And then, when I was about ten, I met my godmother in the forest one day. It was my tenth birthday. Nobody knows this—except you.

PRINCE. Except us.

PRINCESS. Except us. And she told me what her gift meant. It meant that I *was* beautiful—but everybody else was to go on being ignorant, and thinking me plain, until my wedding-day. Because, she said, she didn't want me to grow up spoilt and wilful and vain, as I should have done if everybody had always been saying how beautiful I was ; and the best thing in the world, she said, was to be quite sure of yourself, but not to expect admiration from other people. So ever since then my mirror has told me I'm beautiful, and everybody else thinks me ugly, and I get a lot of fun out of it.

PRINCE. Well, seeing that Dulcibella is the result, I can only say that your godmother was very, very wise.

PRINCESS. And now tell me *your* secret.

PRINCE. It isn't such a pretty one. You see, Prince Simon was going to woo Princess Camilla, and he'd heard that she was beautiful and haughty and imperious—all *you* would have been if your godmother hadn't been so wise. And being a very ordinary-looking fellow himself, he was afraid she wouldn't think much of him, so he suggested to one of his attendants, a man called Carlo, of extremely attractive appearance, that *he* should pretend to be the Prince, and win the Princess' hand ; and then at the last moment they would change places——

PRINCESS. How would they do that ?

PRINCE. The Prince was going to have been married in full armour—with his visor down.

PRINCESS (*laughing happily*). Oh, what fun !

PRINCE. Neat, isn't it ?

PRINCESS (*laughing*). Oh, very . . . very . . . very.

PRINCE. Neat, but not so terribly *funny*. Why do you keep laughing ?

PRINCESS. Well, that's another secret.

PRINCE. If it comes to that, *I've* got another one up my sleeve. Shall we exchange again ?

PRINCESS. All right. You go first this time.

PRINCE. Very well. . . . I am not Carlo. (*Standing up and speaking dramatically.*) I am Simon !
—*ow !*

(*He sits down and rubs his leg violently.*)

PRINCESS (*alarmed*). What is it ?

PRINCE. Cramp. (*In a mild voice, still rubbing.*) I was saying that I was Prince Simon.

PRINCESS. Shall I rub it for you ? (*She rubs.*)

PRINCE (*still hopefully*). I am Simon.

PRINCESS. Is that better ?

PRINCE (*despairingly*). I am Simon.

PRINCESS. I know.

PRINCE. How did you know ?

PRINCESS. Well, you told me.

PRINCE. But oughtn't you to swoon or something ?

PRINCESS. Why ? History records many similar ruses.

PRINCE (*amazed*). Is that so ? I've never read history. I thought I was being profoundly original.

PRINCESS. Oh, no ! Now I'll tell you *my* secret.
For reasons very much like your own the Princess
Camilla, who is held to be extremely plain, feared
to meet Prince Simon. Is the drawbridge down
yet ?

PRINCE. Do your people give a faint, surprised
cheer every time it gets down ?

PRINCESS. Naturally.

PRINCE. Then it came down about three minutes
ago.

PRINCESS. Ah ! Then at this very moment your
man Carlo is declaring his passionate love for my
maid, Dulcibella. That, I think, is funny. (*So does
the* PRINCE. *He laughs heartily.*) Dulcibella, by the
way, is in love with a man she calls Eg, so I hope
Carlo isn't getting carried away.

PRINCE. Carlo is married to a girl he calls " the
little woman," so Eg has nothing to fear.

PRINCESS. By the way, I don't know if you heard,
but I said, or as good as said, that I am the Princess
Camilla.

PRINCE. I wasn't surprised. History, of which I
read a great deal, records many similar ruses.

PRINCESS (*laughing*). Simon !

PRINCE (*laughing*). Camilla ! (*He stands up.*)
May I try holding you again ? (*She nods. He takes
her in his arms and kisses her.*) Sweetheart !

PRINCESS. You see, when you lifted me up before,
you said, " You're very lovely," and my godmother
said that the first person to whom I would seem
lovely was the man I should marry ; so I knew then
that you were Simon and I should marry you.

PRINCE. I knew directly I saw you that I should
marry you, even if you were Dulcibella. By the way,
which of you *am* I marrying ?

PRINCESS. When she lifts her veil, it will be
Camilla. (*Voices are heard outside.*) Until then it
will be Dulcibella.

PRINCE (*in a whisper*). Then good-bye, Camilla,
until you lift your veil.

PRINCESS. Good-bye, Simon, until you raise your visor.

(*The* KING *and* QUEEN *come in arm-in-arm, followed by* CARLO *and* DULCIBELLA, *also arm-in-arm. The* CHANCELLOR *precedes them, walking backwards, at a loyal angle.*)

PRINCE (*supporting the* CHANCELLOR *as an accident seems inevitable*). Careful!

(*The* CHANCELLOR *turns indignantly round.*)

KING. Who and what is this? More accurately who and what are all these?

CARLO. My attendant, Carlo, Your Majesty. He will, with Your Majesty's permission, prepare me for the ceremony.

(*The* PRINCE *bows.*)

KING. Of course, of course!

QUEEN (*to* DULCIBELLA). Your maid, Dulcibella, is it not, my love? (DULCIBELLA *nods violently.*) I thought so. (*To* CARLO) *She* will prepare Her Royal Highness.

(*The* PRINCESS *curtsies.*)

KING. Ah, yes. Yes. *Most* important.

PRINCESS (*curtsying*). I beg pardon, Your Majesty, if I've done wrong, but I found the gentleman wandering——

KING (*crossing to her*). Quite right, my dear, quite right. (*He pinches her cheek, and takes advantage of this kingly gesture to say in a loud whisper*) We've pulled it off!

(*They sit down ; the* KING *and* QUEEN *on their thrones,* DULCIBELLA *on the* PRINCESS' *throne.* CARLO *stands behind* DULCIBELLA, *the* CHANCELLOR *on the* R. *of the* QUEEN, *and the* PRINCE *and* PRINCESS *behind the long seat on the left.*)

CHANCELLOR (*consulting documents*). H'r m ! Have
I Your Majesty's authority to put the final test to
His Royal Highness ?

QUEEN (*whispering to* KING). Is this safe ?

KING (*whispering*). Perfectly, my dear. I told
him the answer a minute ago. (*Over his shoulder to*
CARLO.) Don't forget. Dog. (*Aloud.*) Proceed,
Your Excellency. It is my desire that the affairs
of my country should ever be conducted in a strictly
constitutional manner.

CHANCELLOR (*oratorically*). By the constitution of
the country, a suitor to Her Royal Highness' hand
cannot be deemed successful until he has given the
correct answer to a riddle. (*Conversationally.*) The
last suitor answered incorrectly, and thus failed to
win his bride.

KING. By a coincidence he fell into the moat.

CHANCELLOR (*to* CARLO). I have now to ask Your
Royal Highness if you are prepared for the ordeal ?

CARLO (*cheerfully*). Absolutely.

CHANCELLOR. I may mention, as a matter, pos-
sibly, of some slight historical interest to our visitor,
that by the constitution of the country the same
riddle is not allowed to be asked on two successive
occasions.

KING (*startled*). What's that ?

CHANCELLOR. This one, it is interesting to recall,
was propounded exactly a century ago, and we must
take it as a fortunate omen that it was well and
truly solved.

KING (*to* QUEEN). I may want my sword directly.

CHANCELLOR. The riddle is this. What is it which
has four legs and mews like a cat ?

CARLO (*promptly*). A dog.

KING (*still more promptly*). Bravo, bravo ! (*He
claps loudly and nudges the* QUEEN, *who claps too.*)

CHANCELLOR (*peering at his documents*). According
to the records of the occasion to which I referred,
the correct answer would seem to be——

PRINCESS (*to* PRINCE). Say something, quick !

CHANCELLOR. —not dog, but——

PRINCE. Your Majesty, have I permission to speak? Naturally His Royal Highness could not think of justifying himself on such an occasion, but I think that with Your Majesty's gracious permission, I could——

KING. Certainly, certainly.

PRINCE. In our country, we have an animal to which we have given the name "dog," or, in the local dialect of the more mountainous districts, "doggie." It sits by the fireside and purrs.

CARLO. That's right. It purrs like anything.

PRINCE. When it needs milk, which is its staple food, it mews.

CARLO (*enthusiastically*). Mews like nobody's business.

PRINCE. It also has four legs.

CARLO. One at each corner.

PRINCE. In some countries, I understand, this animal is called a "cat." In one distant country to which His Royal Highness and I penetrated it was called by the very curious name of "hippopotamus."

CARLO. That's right. (*To the* PRINCE.) Do you remember that ginger-coloured hippopotamus which used to climb on to my shoulder and lick my ear?

PRINCE. I shall never forget it, sir. (*To the* KING.) So you see, Your Majesty——

KING. Thank you. I think that makes it perfectly clear. (*Firmly to the* CHANCELLOR.) You are about to agree?

CHANCELLOR. Undoubtedly, Your Majesty. May I be the first to congratulate His Royal Highness on solving the riddle so accurately?

KING. You may be the first to see that all is in order for an immediate wedding.

CHANCELLOR. Thank you, Your Majesty. (*He bows and withdraws.*)

(*The* KING *rises, as do the* QUEEN *and* DULCIBELLA.)

KING (*to* CARLO). Doubtless, Prince Simon, you

will wish to retire and prepare yourself for the ceremony.

CARLO. Thank you, sir.

PRINCE. Have I Your Majesty's permission to attend His Royal Highness ? It is the custom of his country for Princes of the royal blood to be married in full armour, a matter which requires a certain adjustment——

KING. Of course, of course.

(CARLO *bows to the* KING *and* QUEEN *and goes out. As the* PRINCE *is about to follow, the* KING *stops him.*)

Young man, you have a quality of quickness which I admire. It is my pleasure to reward it in any way which commends itself to you.

PRINCE. Your Majesty is ever gracious. May I ask for my reward *after* the ceremony ? (*He catches the eye of the* PRINCESS, *and they give each other a secret smile.*)

KING. Certainly.

(*The* PRINCE *bows and goes out.*)

(*To* DULCIBELLA.) Now, young woman, make yourself scarce. You've done your work excellently, and we will see that you and your—what was his name ?

DULCIBELLA. Eg, Your Majesty.

KING. —that you and your Eg are not forgotten.

DULCIBELLA. Coo ! (*She curtsies and goes out.*)

PRINCESS (*calling*). Wait for me, Dulcibella !

KING (*to* QUEEN). Well, my dear, we may congratulate ourselves. As I remember saying to somebody once, " You have not lost a daughter, you have gained a son." How does he strike you ?

QUEEN. Stupid.

KING. They made a very handsome pair, I thought, he and Dulcibella.

QUEEN. Both stupid.

KING. I said nothing about stupidity. What I *said* was that they were both extremely handsome.

That is the important thing. (*Struck by a sudden idea.*) Or isn't it ?

QUEEN. What do *you* think of Prince Simon, Camilla ?

PRINCESS. I adore him. We shall be so happy together.

KING. Well, of course you will. I told you so. Happy ever after.

QUEEN. Run along now and get ready.

PRINCESS. Yes, mother. (*She throws a kiss to them and goes out.*)

KING (*anxiously*). My dear, have we been wrong about Camilla all this time ? It seemed to me that she wasn't looking *quite* so plain as usual just now. Did *you* notice anything ?

QUEEN (*carelessly*). Just the excitement of the marriage.

KING (*relieved*). Ah, yes, that would account for it.

CURTAIN.

Lightning Source UK Ltd.
Milton Keynes UK
UKHW020953110422
401398UK00006B/479